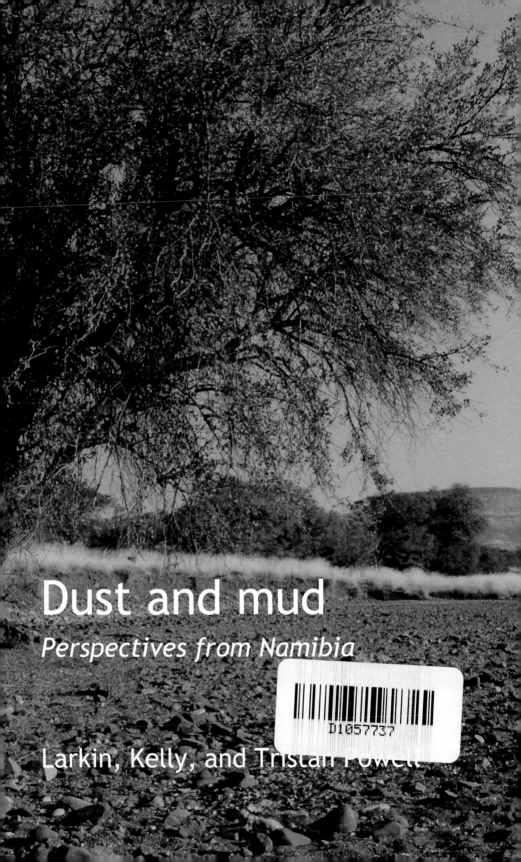

Dust and mud

Perspectives from Namibia

Larkin, Kelly, and Tristan Powell

Table of Contents

Perspectives

Namibian folk stories

Perspectives

When I met his mother

I could guess
You do the work of two men.
I could guess
The cows come when you call them to milking.
I could guess
Bad years have outnumbered the good.
I could guess
You let your grandbabies eat first.
I could guess
Your door is always open.
I could guess
That you only cry at funerals.
I could guess
That you miss him.
I could guess.
But your hands told me.

--L. Powell, on the #Khoadi //Hoas conservancy

Sacred fires

Each morning, the eldest in the village adds wood to the sacred fire. A fire that never goes out. Their offering of scarce firewood makes the fire the center of society. A fire that connects the family to their ancestors. They gather around the fire to pray to their ancestors for guidance. They gather to grieve and to celebrate. The fire smolders through the night as the stars in the sky above mirror the collective fires across the landscape. Thousands of fires. Billions of stars.

Five hundred years ago a little bushman climbed a kopje and spent the evening scratching the outline of a giraffe on the sandstone. When he was finished, he laid down on the warm rock and watched stars fall in the sky. As the moon rose, his fire died and he fell asleep.

Two thousand years ago a group of bushmen gathered under a rock and began to paint. Maybe they were describing a dream or recording a great hunt. As they ate their evening meal, the sun set over the Brandberg.  The smoke from their fire made black streaks on the rocks. The Milky Way swirled above them.

Four to five million years ago the climate changed in southern Africa. Forests disappeared, and grasslands expanded. Paleontologists tell us that this is the event that spawned the incredible diversity of antelope. Grassland expansion may have also responsible for the dramatic evolutionary event which resulted in several species of hominids, standing erect to efficiently carry food across the plains. We can imagine an evening somewhere in an African grassland when a group of *Australopithecus afarensis* sat watching a group of *Australopithecus africanus* pass over the crest of a nearby hill. Both groups spent the night under the stars. Both groups used the full moon to find food.

Today, we look at the stars around our campfire, and they seem to suck the breath from our hearts into the heavens to mix with the souls who have viewed the skies before us. Eyes glistening, reflecting some inner satisfaction.

Maybe satisfaction comes from feeling closer to the stars. From having stripped away all that doesn't matter. Now there is less between you and the sky.

Maybe the feeling is realization of how small we are in the space of history. A realization that sacredness has a vast history on the African plains. We share whatever is sacred, whatever makes us whole, with these bushmen and *Australopithecus*.

Gravity works slowly on thoughts sent starwards. But gravity is gravity, and as you stare at the skies, the weight of previous celestial conversations pulls images into your memory.

Eons of star gazers. Souls bare. All under a well-watched sky. A sky full of sacred fires.

Good night.

--L. Powell, After many conversations with many people about the stars and sacred fires in Namibia

Twilight

The shadows grow long in
Afternoon sun.
Stretching to find a place to hide.
Wind makes a final protest
And joins the shadows over the horizon.

The moon appears, perhaps as the stars' scout
In the near-dark.
And soon the stars gather the courage
To step forward.

The crickets encourage the sun.
"Time to go."
And, like a stage-struck ballerina
Flitting back and back and back
For just one last bow,
The sun is gone.

--L. Powell, Helmeringhausen

Babel babble

The room echoes conversations,
and they pour into my corner of the
papa.
They are in love and on vacation.
He is alone and shouts at the football
match on TV.
They are workers and have many
stories.

She is cooking, and calls to her
husband, the bar tender.
The words slide around chairs.
Behind the bar.
Under the stove.
Slippery words, like greased eels.
They are there and then quickly gone.
Disappearing beyond my reach.
Like trying to sort a pile of bolts into
bins by size,
I struggle to find places to put the
words.
My mind grasps at syllables.
Maybe the lovers need to find red
shoes tomorrow? Probably not.

Perhaps Mr. Lonely thinks the goal
tender is sick?
I'm not sure.
The workers both hurt their thumbs
today?
My best guess.
Did she just run out of salt?
Surely not.
I think of the story of the blind men and the elephant.
I'm only touching the tail of these conversations

Short timer

The dog
looks at me and wags its tail.
Ribs showing.
He lets me scratch between the ticks on his ears.
He leans on my knee.
Drooling.
His look seems to tell me:
Go Home.

--L. Powell, near Ervee

Dust and mud

Dust covers Africa
until the rains come.
Men with white feet.
Ladies in blue dresses with a light hem.
Children run as the elephants cover shattered trees with a
layer of grey.
A donkey shakes and sends clouds into a clear sky.

Rains wash the leaves, and the tree is green again.
White feet turn red.
The donkey's coat is caked near its tail.
The elephants leave and
the dresses are smeared with the past.

--L. Powell, in Kamanjab

On the edge of the Namib

Days of dust.
Dry days.
A cloud, and a smile.
Cattle. Counting the ribs as a countdown to death.
Crowding waterpoints.
An endless valley to search for good grasses.
A valley reminding every cow
It should have been born a goat or an oryx or a springbok.
Like a rabbit from a hat
Springbok pull greenness from dry grass that cattle pass.
And, then the springbok are gone.
Scrambling under fences
Away from cattle and goats.
Secreting to camps of pale green
Hidden where farmers don't go.
The scent of rain, and springbok herds move

Cattle watch behind fences as the horizon
Steals the clouds.
Dry days.

Good years, every so often.
A reason to stay.
A reason to push through droughts.
Years for growth and building
While there is money.
And then, without grass
The money goes away.
Survival.

Dry days.
Rocks make feet stronger
But shoes wear out faster.
Droughts make good neighbors
Who wait for rain together.
Bad years build stamina, character
And every drink of water tastes sweeter.

Miles from electricity
The stars tell bedtime stories.
The Namib makes men strong and smart
And makes smiles rare.
Lonely valleys build strong towns.
No churches but hotels
With big lawns and shade trees
And Saturday night dances.

Dry days.
Life on the edge.
Together.

--J. Powell Helmeringhausen

The road to Maltahöhe

Racing. My truck flies over stones.
Airborne as we come out of rainwashed ravines.
Towards Maltahöhe.

Uphill. All the way we climb
Through the wash plains of the plateau to the southeast.
The book says when Gondwana broke up and South
America
Moved away from Africa
The edge of the continent lifted.
Free of Argentina. Free of Brazil.
Lighter. Floating on magma.
Then, the rains, eons of rains. And winds, eons of winds
Carved this lip, this newly freed land.
Now, plateaus make stairsteps toward the ocean
And rivers of rocks run to meet the sea.

Counting. I keep track of the years as I drive.
Layers in the plateau.
Ocean, desert, ocean.
Sand, limestone, sand.
Climbing. we pass through millions of years, surely,
As the road rises.
Towards Maltahöhe.

Contemplating. Why am I racing?
Isn't this country to explore?
But, the rivers of rocks and carved stone suggest
What can happen if you stand still in this country.
The wind and the rain.
I listen to the rocks of the plateau and the wind gusting on
my truck.
Still speeding
Towards Maltahöhe.

Aha, I say, as I see him.
I knew it, the rocks told the truth.
A farmer fixing the fence.
Living here on gravel plains beneath the plateau.
His forearms scarred like the cliffs, perhaps *Acacia* trees or
barbed wire?
His face furrowed and tanned like sandstone. The sun and
the wind.
His hands gnarled like a twisting, dead tree, grasping wire.
Pushing posts through rock.
His leg misshapen like the valley. Perhaps a run-in with a
leopard or a fall from horseback?
Look what this valley can do to a man.
I wave and push faster.
Towards Maltahöhe.

Escaping. I reach the town.
Atop the plateau.
Away from wind and rocks.
The streets are teaming with more farmers
Bartering for fencing and supplies.
Limping, twisted, slowed. The entire lot marked by the
land.
I slow to watch.

Understanding. It is their way.
To push back against the wind and the rain.
To try to tame the veld.
To argue with Nature.
To stand in the middle of endless time.
To know your fate will be decided by the elements.
To shout at the cliffs.
Scarred, moved, and beaten.
A record of a life lived.
Really lived.
A life recorded on forearms, hands, and faces.
Envious. I want to go back
And drive slowly.
To stop and fix fence.
To stand under the plateau in the wind.
To live.
To live on the road to Maltahöhe.

--L. Powell, near Maltahöhe

Don't you wish you had one of these?

From the far reaches of Windhoek
On the banks of the Meeter
Comes a small bird, a trim bird
Called the Seedonfloor Eater.

The Seedonfloor Eater
Is a Kitchen Floor Cleaner.
It nests in a hole
Of a tree called a Squeener.

An Eater can go months
Without eating a thing.
But once it finds a new floor
The dinner bell rings.

An Eater will clean up
A floor for you quickly.
It flies in and finds crumbs
It's really quite nifty.

Not everyone's kitchen
Can satisfy an Eater.
It takes crumbs that are too big
For mice or mosquiters.

If your kitchen needs cleaning,
Then try calling an Eater.
They come to the sound
Of trumpets and beaters.

Just beat your big beater
And trump your big trumpet
If you play loud he may come
If you offer a crumpet.

The Seedonfloor Eater
Is such a rare bird.
If you get one just stand there.
Don't utter a word.

For the Seedonfloor Eater
Is a valuable addition
To the housecleaning efforts
In any subdivision.

So if your name's Johnny
Or Suzie or Peter.
I know you will want to get
A Seedonfloor Eater.

--L. Powell, in our kitchen in Windhoek, watching 'Freddy the Freeloader' clean our floor.
With apologies to Dr. Seuss.

The oblivious ant

It was an ant.
Carrying a grass seed late in winter.
Lucky to find the seed on the bare ground.

The men sitting in a circle around the ant
did not notice the struggle to carry the seed.
The ant, also oblivious, saw their legs as
giant tree trunks in a forest that needed traversing.

But, the men were making decisions.
Decisions about grass.
Decisions about ants.
Although the men said their decisions were about cattle and
goats.

The men shuffled their feet, debating.
The ant dodged their feet,
worrying only about its cargo and final
destination.

It was the mouths of the men (not their
feet) that decided the ant's fate.
The ant heard only the wind as the men
talked and talked.
Leaving the circle with its seed,
only 12,654 steps to go to reach its mound.

There was no vote.
Only nodding heads.
The men decided that the ant, next year,
would have more seeds.

Then, the circle dissolved. Back to work.
The ant handed off its seed, and turned
back to the veld.
Back to work.
To find more seeds.

--L. Powell, on the Ehirovipuka
Conservancy

Walls of my apartheid

I went to the market
And spent more on groceries for a week
Than he makes in a month.
He came to the car as I left
With his hand out.
I paid him 50 cents,
Because he had guarded my car
From those who make even less.

When I paid and reclaimed responsibility for my own car
The others came. Selling. Please sir.
Beaded frogs. New knives. A necklace.
Nothing I needed, sorry.
A lady with a sign. Deaf.
Please give. Maybe she could hear me sigh.

Driving home, I pass two guys
Trying to stop cars to sell
Feather dusters.
My gate slides shut behind my car.
Safe. No one reaching into my pocket.

I hear the snap of my electric fence.
Safe. Easy.
Walls that allow me to breathe.
To ignore.

But, I understand.
Without the walls, I have to
Watch them. I have to hear them.
My walls.

Every week, I slip out and put the garbage on the curb.
Then, I go inside and let the wall hide them
As they go through the refuse.

nderstand.
e people who built the walls were not evil.
ey were not hateful.
ey were tired.
ey just wanted to go to the market.

eir market.
eir walls.

Powell, in Windhoek

Hunting with Orion

It was a nice surprise to see Orion when we arrived in
Namibia,
Although the image of the hunter plunging headlong with
his sword into the night sky was odd.
A world upside-down.

But, regardless of angle, we had a friend in this new land.
A sun-loving celestial body who had joined us on our
journey from frigid North America for more southerly
pursuits.

Only in the southern hemisphere does Orion promise
warmth and long days.
And he was true to his word.
Until, one night, we searched and realized we'd been left
alone. No hunter to guard our night skies.

Winter. Planning evenings around when we could use the
space heater or how long we could stand cold tile on our
feet until escaping into piles of blankets.
A warm bed. A long winter with unfriendly stars.
Orion was hiding behind the sun and even the sun is shy
during winter.

Last week, we looked up and realized our friend had
returned.
The hunter had found us, and with him came warmth, rain,
and longer days.

But we were like the houseguest who stops by to break your
morning and then tells you she must leave because she has
something much more important to do than to talk to you.
Orion was back. A reminder to us that we had to leave.
To apologize while walking backwards.
To travel north long after the birds have gone south.

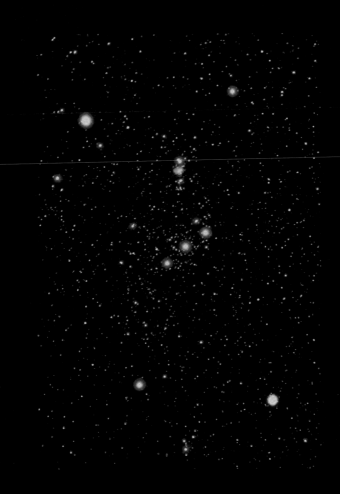

But, still, with Orion.
Our connection between grassland and bushveld.
A messenger between worlds.

And so, we will sit in the cold and we will dream of summer.
We will dream of hunting with Orion.

--L. Powell, Otjiwarongo

Image of the Orion constellation from the Hubble Space Telescope collection. Image is available for use in the public domain through the efforts of NASA and the Space Telescope Science Institute.

Namibia in the morning

light coming through the window
bacon in the pan
children singing "Namibia"
happy because it's one day closer to coming home
the nice cool air
seeing my friends again

--Tristan Powell, back home in Lincoln, NE

Namibian folk stories

The parable of the python and the cigarette

There was a man who needed to build a house. He was gathering reeds in the river in a wooden canoe. He was doing well until a python fell into his boat.

He couldn't jump into the river, because the crocodiles would get him. So, he was stuck out on the tip of his canoe as the python came closer and closer.

The man saw his friend in a canoe down the river. He knew that he couldn't ask him to come save him from the python, because his friend would be scared of the python. His friend would never come save him.

So, he asked his friend to come give him a light for his cigarette. The friend came, and the man quickly jumped onto his friend's boat and was saved from the python.

--As told by Christopher, who was explaining how it is often hard to tell people why you are asking for help.

Stealing

In the north of Namibia, we do not steal. If you steal a goat, and the guy comes to ask you if you have seen the goat, you should just tell him, "I took your goat." Because if you lie to him, he can witch you and that night the goat (which you have eaten) inside of you will start talking. And you will start to talk like a goat. Baaaaa-aaaaa!

If you steal a goat and want to go home by going around the mountain, you will instead always come back to where you started. You will not be able to go home.

If you are sick and a witch doctor comes, he will ask you for money. He will witch the money and tell you to throw it away. So, if someone finds the money on the ground and takes it, they will also take your sickness away. Because of this, everyone* knows not to take money they find lying on the ground!

--As told by Peter, sharing why people in the Caprivi region do not steal

The Tokoloshi

I wanted to marry a girl, by my parents did not approve of her. They told me I should not marry her. Regardless, I decided to work up the courage to ask her parents if I could marry her. According to our tradition, I went to live with the girl and her parents for one year. I made houses of reeds for them, and I planted and harvested a mahangu [corn] field.

After the year was over, I decided to take the girl to be my wife, and her parents approved of me. We left to go to our new home. Her parents gave us a basket of mahangu and a goat.

The first day after we were at our new home, I was out in the woods with my brother-in-law. We found a hole in the ground, and there was a very short man standing next to it. My brother-in-law was scared and said it was the Tokoloshi, and he ran away. I was not scared, but soon I also decided he was the Tokoloshi, and I also ran. He followed me back to my house.

I went inside my house and realized that my wife could not see the Tokoloshi. I tried to explain what had happened, but she could not see. The short man grabbed a cup and plate from the table and dropped it on the floor. My wife thought I had thrown them on the floor. "No," I said. "It is the short man who followed me home."

The next day dawned, and my wife also saw the short man. She was frightened, and we decided to go to her parents house. As we left, the short man followed us.

"Take me with you," he demanded.

"No," we responded. "You cannot come."

Well, at least take me back to the hole in the ground where you found me," he said. We agreed, and we took him to his hole on our donkey cart.

When we reached his hole, he demanded his share of our basket of mahangu. We were scared of him, so we gave him half of the mahangu.

"What about the goat?" the short man asked. So, we gave him the goat. He took his knife and killed it and cut it in half.

"Let's go," I told my wife

"Wait," said the short man. "What about your wife?"

"You cannot have my wife," I replied. But, the short man grabbed my wife, took his knife, killed her and cut her in half.

I ran screaming through the woods to my parents' house. When I got there I told my parents the story.

My parents led me to the next room. There was my wife, alive and whole. Also, the goat and the full basket of mahangu.

"We told you we did not approve of this woman," my parents told me. "Now, look what the ghosts are telling you. Take her home to her parents and leave her."

And, I did.

The authors and photographers

Larkin, Kelly, and Tristan Powell traveled to Namibia
during January to December, 2009 to participate in a
Fulbright Scholar program at Polytechnic of Namibia in
Windhoek, Namibia. Larkin taught courses in Natural
Resource Management, and Kelly volunteered with several
groups that support orphans and vulnerable children.
Tristan (12) attended the Windhoek International School.

The Powell's traveled extensively during the year, and
enjoyed time to think and contemplate the adventure
around them.